Russia

Jenny Vaughan and Chris Barnard

STECK-VAUGHN
L I B R A R Y
A Division of Steck-Vaughn Company

Hello! My name is Tanya.
I live in Leningrad.
Leningrad is a big city in Russia.

2

I live in these apartments with my family.
Our apartment is on the top floor.
We can see the city of Leningrad
from our windows.

This is my grandmother.
We call her Baboushka, which
is Russian for Grandmother.
She takes care of my brother Yuri and me
when Mom and Dad are at work.

Baboushka takes us to school
on the trolley bus.
There are many trolley buses
in Leningrad.

This is my school.

We go to school every morning.

We don't have school in the afternoon.

6

In the afternoon we sometimes go to
the Palace of Pioneers.
We can sing, dance, and play
different games there.

There are many rivers and
canals in Leningrad, so
there are many bridges
over the canals, too.

Sometimes we take a boat trip
around the canals.
Tourists like to go on these boats.
It is a good way to see Leningrad.

It is very cold here in the winter.
The canals freeze, and there is ice
on the Neva River.

We wear many clothes to keep warm
when we play outside.

People play ice hockey in the winter
and skate on the frozen ponds.

Parts of the sea freeze in the winter, too.
People make holes in the ice and
try to catch fish through the holes.

There is plenty of snow, too.
People like to go skiing or
sledding in the snow.
Sometimes we have a ride in
a horse-drawn sled called a troika.

But even when it is very cold,
Russian people still like
to eat ice cream!

My little brother Yuri likes
to play in the snow.
Here he is on our sled.
Mom has made sure that
he is wearing his warm clothes!

16

In the summer, we don't have to
wear so many clothes.
The weather is often sunny and warm.
When it is nice we like to visit
Leningrad's famous art galleries
and museums.

Leningrad was once the capital of Russia.
In those days, it was called St. Petersburg.
Many kings and queens lived here
in their palaces.
Russian kings were called czars.

Peter the Great was a famous
czar of Russia.
He built the Peter Paul Fortress, which
you can still see in Leningrad today.
I like the dungeons in the fortress where
he used to keep prisoners.

The czars had a huge winter palace.
Now it is part of the Hermitage Museum.
The Hermitage has many beautiful paintings
and furniture inside.

20

Peter had a summer palace, too.
This is the garden of the Summer Palace.
In the winter all of the statues are
covered up to protect them from the cold.

In the summer the czars liked to go
to the country.
Peter built another palace outside
Leningrad called Peterhof.

One day in summer, we went to visit Peterhof.
The trip was arranged by the Young Pioneers,
which is a club for children.
We all wear red scarves and red caps.

Peterhof is close to the river,
so we went there by boat
from Leningrad.

As we went down the river, we saw
the famous old Russian warship, the "Aurora,"
which is tied up in the Neva River.

When we arrived, we walked to the palace.
It has statues and
fountains in the gardens.
We all liked the Grand Cascade with
its waterfall and golden statues.

We walked around the gardens
and saw all the different
fountains and waterfalls.
The dragons at the top of this waterfall
spout water from their mouths.

This fountain is shaped like a mushroom.

Children like to run through the water.

They try not to get wet!

One of my friends sat down on a white bench.
He wondered why people laughed at him.
He soon found out because when
he sat down, a fountain shot up.
It was a trick fountain, and he got very wet!

Then we went inside the palace and
looked at the beautiful decorations
and furniture.
This is a picture of the throne room
of the czars.

In the dining room, we saw
the white-and-gold dinner plates and
bowls that once belonged to the czar.
We also saw beautiful paintings and
furniture.

When we came out of the palace,
we listened to a band playing Russian tunes.
Then it was time to go back to Leningrad
on the boat.

Index

NOTE TO THE READER:
In this book we talk about the country Russia. Leningrad is part of Russia.
Russia is part of a much bigger country called the Soviet Union or the
U.S.S.R. People often use the name Russia to mean the whole bigger
country, too.

Reading Consultant: Diana Bentley
Editorial Consultant: Donna Bailey
Supervising Editor: Kathleen Fitzgibbon

Illustrated by Gill Tomblin
Picture research by Suzanne Williams
Designed by Richard Garratt Design

Photographs
Cover: Robert Harding Picture Library
Bruce Coleman: 10 (Michael Freeman), 23 (Normal Myers),
    3, 31 (Jonathan T. Wright)
Colorific: 4, 24, 27, 28
Format: 6 (Brenda Price)
Robert Harding Picture Library: 20, 26, 30, 32
The Hutchison Library: 1, 12, 14, 16
Novosti Press Agency: 8, 9, 11, 22
Remote Source: 25 (N. Allsop)
Rex Features: 7, 13, 15
David Williamson: 17, 21 (Andrzej Jaroszewicz)
ZEFA: 5

Library of Congress Cataloging-in-Publication Data: Vaughan, Jenny. [Russia] Russia / Jenny Vaughan and
Chris Barnard; [illustrated by Gill Tomblin]. p. cm. —(Where we live) Previously published as: We live in
Russia. SUMMARY: A brief descriptive tour of Leningrad. ISBN 0-8114-2549-5 1. Leningrad (R.S.F.S.R.)—
Description—Juvenile literature. [1. Leningrad (R.S.F.S.R.)—Description.] I. Barnard, Chris,
1952– . II. Tomblin, Gill, ill. III. Title. IV. Series. DK552.V38   1990   914.7′453—dc20   89-26121
CIP   AC

1 2 3 4 5 6 7 8 9 LB 96 95 94 93 92 91 90